Food Stories For Beginning Food Entrepreneurs About Food Service Businesses & Opportunities For Beginners, Food Service Business Ideas, Product Ideas & Catering

Beginner's Crafts Guide Series

Mary Kay Patterson

Published by InfinitYou, 2017.

While every precaution has been taken in the preparation of this book, the publisher assumes no responsibility for errors or omissions, or for damages resulting from the use of the information contained herein.

FOOD STORIES FOR BEGINNING FOOD ENTREPRENEURS ABOUT FOOD SERVICE BUSINESSES & OPPORTUNITIES FOR BEGINNERS, FOOD SERVICE BUSINESS IDEAS, PRODUCT IDEAS & CATERING

First edition. July 4, 2017.

Copyright © 2017 Mary Kay Patterson.

ISBN: 978-1386449607

Written by Mary Kay Patterson.

Introduction

Do you love food or are you a foody?

If you are a foody and if you are passionate about food, you will love this guide because it shows you the 8 absolute most unique and creative ways of how to make some serious cash with food deliciousness!

Food books have never been more enjoyable and satisfying like this food business guide because it shows everyone who has a passion for food how to make a true profitable food business out of it!

In this guide you will learn about the secretly guarded from passion to profit secret ingredients that you must absolutely know about if food is your true hobby.

This guide is chock full of the best food business techniques, know-how, resources, and food marketing strategies that are used by today's "Food Elite".

Use these secret food tips and knowledge immediately to make profits today! The guide will reveal the secret ingredients that you need in order to achieve a successful food venture.

The report covers unique ways to profit from food like "Exotic Food Creation Profits", "Profitable Fancy Cookbook Secrets", "Foody Best Selling Author", and lots more exciting ways how to make profit from food goodness ASAP!

Once these secrets are in your hands, you can start impressing your family and friends with your new-found from passion to profit food knowledge.

Pick up this guide to finally discover what the "Food Elite" has been secretly hiding for years. Impress the foody community around you with some mentally stimulating and enjoyable food nuggets.

In summary, this guide introduces you to the most unique ways of profiting from food, and it let's you know about all the beneficial from passion to profit ways that will help you achieve the ultimate lifestyle!

You will know about 8 easy to consume and apply eye-opening food business stories told by some of the most authoritative food experts and food entrepreneurs that are part of today's food elite because they have all turned their food passion into food profits.

Not only do they show unique ways of how to make it in today's food business world via adding multiple income streams to one's business, but they are also showing the most strategic marketing methods that even a newbie can apply today.

It is even a smarter idea to set up these multiple income streams!

You already love what you are doing with food right?

Talking about bending the advantages to your side!

There is simply no other way to become financially independent as easily and as quickly as this because you already have all the advantages on your side. It is just a matter of turning your passions for food into a profitable food business venture and the knowledge in this guide will do the thinking for you!

All you have to do is take it and then make it!

Let's, go ahead and let's start digging through this guide ASAP.

Run with the knowledge from this guide and become a food celebrity and authority in your own right because this amazing food opportunity is waiting for you!

Make it happen today...

Cook Up Some True Profits

A few months ago, another of my foody friends who has a true passion for homemade food, started a secret food journal. This experience has led her to a very profitable part time business venture with food that anyone can do.

Yes, my friend Molly who is truly passionate about food has totally figured out how to make huge profits from her love for cooking.

What are Molly's secret ingredients for this lucrative business with food?

Molly identified a very profitable food opportunity and she allowed me to share her food story in this chapter that is all about cooking up some true profits with food.

If you, like Molly, love to experiment and cook food and if your guests and family have been complimenting you throughout the years, telling you how delicious your food is, this food opportunity might be for you. You have the ability to cook up some real profits.

Wanna to learn more?

Ok, let's ask Molly about her secret ingredients that anyone who would love to do this must absolutely know about.

Molly, a mother of two, is cooking supper and I am asking her about her secrets.

I guess cooking supper for one's family is nothing unusual, but Molly happens to be cooking for 7 families.

Moreover, Molly is making good profit from doing so, while staying at home and looking after her 2 children.

Molly tells me that people love home cooked style meals because meals like that remind them of their Mom's cooking. Molly tells me that frozen microwave dinners as well as instant meals have become the reality for a busy family today. Molly however likes to take advantage of this reality and she offers a food alternative for these modern families. Molly is even charging a premium price for doing so.

So listen up if you like Molly enjoy making these delicious meals, an enjoyable food business is not very far away from you.

You will need to decide on a menu first because this is the key to success. Moly chooses meal plans that can very easily be multiplied without sacrificing the quality. These meals should be easy to reheat for the family as well. She is offering some individual options like lasagna, potpies, and a variety of salads to accompany the meal. Molly tells me that one-dish type meals are the simplest to offer. She also cooks up side dishes.

What is Molly's secret tip for coming up with her amazing dishes?

She is using the power of the internet for her research.

She is using sites like:

allrecipes.com[1]
therecipewebsite.com[2]
foodhistory.com[3]
free-gourmet-recipes.com[4]
recipetrove.com[5]
recipesecrets.net/forums[6]
recipesupersource.com[7]
epicurious.com[8]
foodnetwork.com[9]
foodily.com[10]
supercook.com[11]
punchfork.com[12]
yummly.com[13]

---

1. http://www.allrecipes.com
2. http://www.therecipewebsite.com
3. http://www.foodhistory.com
4. http://www.free-gourmet-recipes.com
5. http://www.recipetrove.com
6. http://www.recipesecrets.net/forums
7. http://www.recipesupersource.com
8. http://www.epicurious.com
9. http://www.foodnetwork.com
10. http://www.foodily.com
11. http://www.supercook.com
12. http://www.punchfork.com
13. http://www.yummly.com

FOOD STORIES FOR BEGINNING FOOD ENTREPRENEURS ABOUT FOOD SERVICE BUSINESSES & OPPORTUNITIES FOR BEGINNERS, FOOD SERVICE BUSINESS IDEAS, PRODUCT IDEAS & CATERING

http://shine.yahoo.com/food

Molly plans menus by the week, or month. She also offers one or two meal options per day.

She is using advertising from her local paper and she uses door-to-door advertising via flyers that she orders from a site called Fiverr.com. She only pays local students $5 for distributing her flyers at some strategic points in her local community.

She gives out her daily menu plans to everyone she meets during the day and she always includes her daily meal proposals together with her business information with each of her orders that go out to her clients.

She includes all her important contact information. She offers a deliver service and her clients can also pick-up the orders.

She uses some very sneaky qr code technology that she has learned from the Zero Cost Marketing go to guy Dan who is a genius when it comes to slashing the costs to run a business to Zero costs.

If you would like to discover how you can slash your own costs of doing business to literally ZERO cost, you can watch Dan's webinar from here[14].

He shows some very sneaky strategies that every entrepreneur should know about.

Molly is using Dan's strategies for everything from using qr codes that she prints on her flyers so that people can scan them with their phones to get her daily menus and some discounts to using his sneaky marketing strategies that involve free advertising via sharing her delicious food and menu photos on a site called Pinterest.com.

She even learned about a method how to charge her clients's credit cards via her iphone when she is delivering her order to them.

Heck, she is not even paying the relatively high commission to paypal anymore because she is using Dan's recommendations. This paypal alternative is killer and using it helps her make even more profits today than ever before.

She tells me that Dan's methods are killer and that he is teaching her the most profitable mobile marketing and coupon marketing strategies that are perfectly integrating with her local food business because her customers are profiting from her mobile optimized technologies in the end.

---

14. http://www.markzuckerbergfortune.info/like/FromPassionToProfit

Another secret ingredient for her business is to use reasonable prices. Her prizes are similar to frozen meal products that are available in the local supermarket. She also offers family discounts and monthly subscriptions to daily meal plans. She offers free bonuses such as cheese sticks, tomato bruschetta, olive oil and garlic bread and some homemade dippings.

She requests that all orders are phoned to her by 4:00 pm and this helps her with the logistics because she will know exactly how much to cook on a day to day basis.

Molly tells me that clients do not pick up their orders on time and therefore the ability to reheat foods is important.

She packages the meals in styrofoam take out type containers and lids. She uses extra bags for larger orders.

She also notes that it is very important to check ones local health regulations before getting started with this type of food business.

She is allowed to do this business because she holds a Health Permit that allows her to sell food.

Depending on where you live, the Health Permit will be issued to you after a quick inspection of your cooking and prep areas. You might be required to take a quick food safety course.

The course is a good idea anyway because it is going to ensure you serve the highest quality food to your customers.

You can check foodsafety.gov for more information on US health standards.

Lastly, she gives me a last good tip. Molly is left with extra food almost daily and she profits from these left overs.

Molly freezes these meals and offers a frozen food section to her line of food meals.

This is yet another additional income stream for her food business and people love her frozen food which boosts additional sales.

Molly has so much success with her frozen food meal products, therefore she is now adding an extra frozen food product line to her food production.

Resources:

http://www.mealsmatter.org[1]
　　http://www.foodsafety.gov
　　Zero Cost Marketing Webinar[2]

---

1. http://www.mealsmatter.org
2. 　http://www.markzuckerbergfortune.info/like/FromPassionToProfit

Lucrative Business Opportunities For Personal Chefs

My friend Glenna is another foody and she loves the concept of from passion to profits. She allowed me to interview her and share all her secret ingredients that make her personal chef business profitable.

I will be sharing Glenna's secret ingredients in this chapter.

If you like Glenna are more at home in your kitchen than any other room in your house, this food opportunity might be for you.

Does the idea of experimenting with locally grown and fresh natural ingredients excite you?

If so, it turns out, you are just the perfect person that many family households are looking for to solve their meal problems.

Most of the families do not have the time to cook a delicious meal for their loved ones. The only real solution to their cooking needs is to hire a personal chef who does the cooking for them.

Many families or singles today are having a problem with meal plans. Although they have a great desire to cook a healthy meal for their family and to avoid fast food places as well as unhealthy prepared meals that are full of chemicals and preservatives, they just do not have the time to do so. Many families resort to daily meal solutions like ordering from the local food delivery services. However this is not a practical long-term food solution to their problems!

This dilemma is Glenna's business opportunity.

As a personal chef, Glenna prepares a set number of meals for a certain number of days during the week. Glenna cooks for dinner parties and other occasions as well. She is discussing the client's personal preferences beforehand and she is then offering the client a personalized daily, weekly, and monthly meal plan that fits the household's bugdet and taste. Most families have the hardest time to prepare dinners after a long day of work. Glenna is scheduling dinners for these families for their weeknight dinner meal plans.

Glenna is only sticking with fresh locally grown and natural foods that are in season. She is saving money on ingredients because she is providing the families she is cooking for with a meal plan that has a very natural and fresh flavor and that is full of vitamins and minerals. She is preparing most of her fresh ingredients a bit in advance. Most of the time she is bringing everything she needs to the location of the client that she is cooking for.

Glenna is doing her cooking in the kitchen of her client. Like this the customer will receive his or her meals steamingly hot and extra fresh and directly from the stove. She tells me that the key is to carefully schedule and prepare the fresh ingredients in advance. She has the ability to do the cooking work for more than one family each night and on any given night.

She is able to buy her ingredients in bulk like the restaurants are doing it because she has a client base. She tells me that buying in bulk is a huge money saver and it is the key to making good profits.

Glenna is also offering her clients another option. She is preparing a full week's worth of fresh and healthy

meals beforehand.

She is then delivering the meals to all her clients at once and her clients in turn are able to reheat the meals whenever it fits their schedule.

She has registered with organizations that do send out personal chefs like Glenna on demand.

She tells me that she has gotten her new personal chef cooking business on its feet and this helped her build up her initial experience and skills that she needs as a personal chef.

Glenna herself has obtained her chef certification with the USPCA (United States Personal Chef Organization).

When he started up her business as a personal chef her first order of business was to help people find her business.

Glenna let the cat out of the bag and tell me about your key to success marketing strategies!

She tells me that she is using plain word of mouth advertising that she got from a Guerilla marketing type book. Glenna reveals that she loves these types of typical Guerilla marketing type strategies because they work for her cooking business.

Using these Guerilla marketing strategies has allowed her to increase her client base in a very short period of time.

Her tip is to search google or the Kindle marketplace for titles like Guerilla marketing. She loves to digest the information in a step by step way. In order to be able to apply these methods, she only reads one chapter per week and applies one strategy into her business each month. Taking things one by one prevents overwhelm and frustration because she is able to give the method enough time to work. Once the marketing method is integrated and working and once she gets motivation out of the results that are coming from this one method, she is moving on with the next idea.

The basis of her marketing consists of printing up flyers and posting them in strategic places where professional cooks and nonprofessional people are hanging out in her local area.

She is also including popular lunch and coffee shop places in her marketing mix.

She takes advantage from the bulletin boards of her local post-offices and grocery stores. She uses any public bulletin boards in her local area to her advantage in order to offer her personal chef services.

Resources:

http://www.hireachef.com[1]
   http://www.fabjob.com/caterer.asp

http://www.uspca.com[2]

http://www.personalchef.com/appca_training_options.php[3]

http://www.personalchef.uk.com[4]

http://www.cpcalliance.com[5]

---

1. http://www.hireachef.com
2. http://www.uspca.com
3. http://www.personalchef.com/appca_training_options.php
4. http://www.personalchef.uk.com
5. http://www.cpcalliance.com

Profitable Fancy Cookbook Secrets

If you love to cook like my friend Diane and you have a couple of hours on your hands then this sure fire way of making a profit with food is absolutely for you.

Diane has always enjoyed cooking for her family and friends and has therefore received hundreds of compliments for her delicious cooking art.

She loves to cook wonderful and chef like meals and has turned her passion into a very profitable fancy cookbook business: She is teaching it!

How did she come up with her food related business idea?

She tells me that everyone loves to receive nice compliments for a wonderful meal. It is also true that most of the people would like to cook delicious meals for their family, but people do not have a clue where to get started with. Fancy cookbook recipes for example are not always the best way to find out about how to cook a delicious and unique meal.

This thinking is what made Diane come up with her own food business idea and that is creating her own fancy cooking lessons.

So what are your secret ingredients for your fancy cooking lesson business Diane?

Diane has a series of delicious dishes up her sleeve and these dishes kind of work like her signature dish line.

She says that every recipe that is a little bit oriented towards the oriental and latino kitchen would be a good and qualifying recipe to be included in such a fancy series of cooking lessons.

She says that everyone who is a foody and has some love for cooking and the kitchen is able to be a

cooking teacher.

All she needs is a kitchen and a place to buy her more exotic ingredients. Lastly, she needs her own recipes and in her case these recipes make up her signature recipe line.

She tells me that if you can cook you can teach as well plus it is a lot of fun to meet new people who all have a passion for food.

What are her secret ingredients for her cooking class marketing?

Diane starts her marketing campaign by putting an ad in her local paper. She also lists her class locally because her area puts out a list of events and classes.

You can also list your class in the Learning Annex. Ask your local schools and universities if they are interested to run this type of cooking class.

Diane is all about multiple streams of income and has figured out many additional ways of distribution. She has made her signature cooking lessons into a physical product that people can order online.

She uses places like Etsy.com, Ebay, Smashwords, and udemy.com to distribute her cooking lessons in the form of ebooks, physical books, and physical DVD courses.

On her own website she is selling her cooking lesson in physical format and she uses a site called Kunaki.

Kunaki is doing all the hard and technical work for her like burning the course onto DVDs and shipping the orders out to customers.

She also uses Amazon via a site called createspace where she is able to turn her cooking lessons into a DVD course and sell it through the Amazon marketplace.

Heck, she is even using her own blog to come up with very valuable daily cooking lessons that people might want to pay for because of the value that she is providing on a day to day basis and she is using her favorite marketplace Amazon to make another cool profit from her blog.

Amazon has a program that gives bloggers like Diane the opportunity to register a blog and then Amazon goes and finds subscribers that are paying for a monthly subscription in order to be able to read the daily updated blog posts of that blog. Diane's blog is registered with that program that Amazon offers.

Diane learned all these sneakiness from our friend Dan the Zero Cost Marketing guy.

She is also using the power of sites like Pinterest where she shares the coolest food pictures that she can come up with. Her target audience will click on the pictures and this leads them to her own courses and products online.

Dan is a true From Zero to Hero type of internet marketer and you can listen to his free webinar where he shares his wizard knowledge.

Check it out here![6]

What else is Diane doing for her marketing?

---

6. http://www.markzuckerbergfortune.info/like/FromPassionToProfit

She is hanging up posters with her detailed class information and her website address. Her site gives them much more details because she is featuring some of her videos from her youtube channel on her site to give people a taste for her classes.

She notes that she is including menus for each class, so that potential students will know exactly what they can learn, a price, and a must-bring list for the class is also mentioned. She is also posting what her student class limit is. Usually she accepts between 1-3 students minimum and not more than 7 students maximum in order to guarantee an exclusive learning experience.

Sometimes if she gets a hold of a space with several sinks and stoves, like a home economics lab in a school, she will make an exception and in this case she will take some more students.

She is planning her menus well ahead of time and she requires her students to preregister for her classes.

Like this she can purchase the correct amount of fresh ingredients at her local farmer's market on the same day as she is teaching her class.

She has several dishes that she can demonstrate in front of the whole class and then she assigns the students to each of the dishes demonstrated earlier. She is offering a sit down meal at the end of each cooking class. Like this she is able to show her students how to present the dishes in a very decorative and artful way. This adds a nice treat to her classes and students love little treats and bonuses like this because it makes her classes very personal and unique. Most of her students come back for advanced cooking classes because Diane masters the art of using a unique selling position and Diane is hooking her students for life.

What a wonderful way to mix ones passion with profit like Diane is mastering it!

Diane tells me that she truly loves her lifestyle and that she can not ask for anything more than what she is doing with her life.

Let's look at some additional tips that Diane is sharing.

Diane is running her cooking classes for around 2 hours. She is testing and timing her recipes first and then she adds about 30 minutes for instruction time.

She is only sticking to recipes that do not include very advanced maneuvers and actions unless she has some students who want to continue her cooking classes.

In this case she builds up her cooking classes to an advanced level over a time period of several weeks.

She is charging her students enough money to be able to cover the costs of her ingredients, her time that is

worth about $30 per hour.

She then multiplies her hourly rate by the number of students. She is charging higher fees for more personalized and individual one on one type cooking classes.

She is also telling her students where they can find special ingredients. She provides a booklet with resources for the ingredients and she provides the recipes in printed version. At the end of the class she tells her students about her subscription website where they can learn up to date cooking tips and tricks and some more of her delicious recipes.

She also shows some examples of her physical courses and hands out her business card with her website and options from where they can buy her line of products online.

She motivates her students at the end of each class to go home and cook the same recipe for their family and to get started with their own recipe journal.

She tells me that she is sometimes holding one-time classes and at other times ongoing ones.

She is also providing the option for her students to pay a monthly fee that includes one or two classes per week, each week building on skills learned the week before.

She is always adding new cooking lesson themes to her line of cooking classes. She offers themes like

Polynesian, Chinese, Indian, Mexican, French, Italian, and German food recipes.

This keeps the students interested and hooked plus it funnels more students into her classes because word of mouth is kicking in as well.

She also motivates her students to bring friends to class and like this she has already doubled her client base.

She also applies coupon and discount marketing that she learned from Dan the Zero Cost Marketing go to guy.

She just schedules more cooking classes in one day once her class takes off like wildfire.

She says that the great thing about cooking classes is that one can really schedule four or five cooking classes per day.

Diane likes the idea from passion into profit and therefore she increases her daily classes and thus her earning potential.

Resources:

http://www.mymommybiz.com/ideas/cookingclass.html[1]
http://www.ehow.com/how_2054510_teach-cooking-class.html
The Learning Annex[2]
Etsy.com[3]
udemy.com[4]
Pinterest.com[5]
Youtube.com[6]
Kunaki.com[7]

---

1. http://www.mymommybiz.com/ideas/cookingclass.html
2. http://learningannex.com
3. http://www.Etsy.com
4. http://www.udemy.com
5. http://www.pinterest.com
6. http://www.youtube.com
7. http://www.kunaki.com

Private Cooking Lesson Profits

Another foody friend of mine Melanie tells me that plotting the weekly dinner menu plan can often be a very difficult task for amateurs.

Don't you think that dishes like lasagna, hamburgers, hot dogs, pizza, meatloaf, and spaghetti can get very boring after a certain time?

If you like Melanie enjoy cooking for your family and friends, you might just have stumbled upon a very viable food business. The private cooking lesson business is allowing you to do what you already love and make profit in the process: a true from passion to profit thinking!

Melanie tells me that most of the people do have time constraints and everybody lacks time. People have hectic days and are stressed out at the end of the day.

Most of the women that come home from work simply do not want to experiment with new dishes; most would rather cook a meal they know is going to be a success, throw something in the microwave or the slow cooker and call this a dinner solution.

Worse some of them go through the drive-thru at a fast food joint on the way home from work.

This is where Melanie's food business idea comes in. She identified a huge business opportunity from those multi-billion dollar fast food restaurant chains.

Melanie's claim is simple. Families or singles will hire you to come to their homes and teach them how to cook a delicious meal.

Melanie is charging between $250 and $350 a week for five nightly cooking lessons.

She is bringing all the ingredients for the meal and the client only has to supply the kitchen, some motivation to learn how to cook, and some enthusiasm for the task at hand.

Melanie loves this business because in home cooking lessons provide the perfect platform to develop some creative meal plans and she can be as creative as she wants.

Melanie for example offers busy people type cooking lessons and she teaches these people who to cook delicious dishes in a very quick and easy way.

FOOD STORIES FOR BEGINNING FOOD ENTREPRENEURS ABOUT FOOD SERVICE BUSINESSES & OPPORTUNITIES FOR BEGINNERS, FOOD SERVICE BUSINESS IDEAS, PRODUCT IDEAS & CATERING

She is offering them a list of alternative dishes and her clients are choosing a weekly meal plan that they would like to cook and learn how to cook in a simple and quick way.

She is also offering family type of cooking lessons. These are cooking lessons that include the whole family and the whole family participates and learns how to cook these delicious family type of dishes. This is perfect to learn from a pro how to cook these wonderful family occasion and holiday type dishes like how to make a turkey for Thanksgiving and how to prepare and cook the perfect Christmas dinner.

She buys her ingredients from the local grocery store and the farmer's or fish market. Do not forget to sign up for some kind of discount or price plus card that most shops and stores offer.

She is saving a lot of money from these savings because she buys a lot of certain type discount products. She always makes sure to check her Sunday newspaper in order to clip some valuable coupons to save money.

What marketing strategies is Melanie using in order to make her from passion into profit business truly lucrative?

She loves her marketing mix simple and uses her free newspapers to place ads for her private cooking classes.

She loves to place ads in the Pennysaver and Craigslist because it simply works.

She uses signs that someone from Fiverr.com is posting for her. Flyers with tear off strips work wonders for her business. She includes her information like her name and phone number. She also profits from the local bulletin boards at places like the local grocery stores, the post office, the hair dresser, and other hang out places where women hang out.

What is her favorite secret marketing strategy?

She uses Zero Cost Marketing type strategies. She contacts her local newspaper and tells them about her from passion into profit business and her entrepreneur spirit in her hometown.

Make your story really newsy and interesting pretty much like a news story that you would love to read about in a newspaper. This will almost all the time make them interested enough about your story and they will most likely write a feature story about you for the next issue.

She also knows that many towns and states do offer business publications. These publications do list all the newest businesses and they also do feature newsworthy articles about passionate entrepreneurs.

Melanie uses the power of the news because being featured as a local entrepreneur in a local newspaper is a very powerful marketing strategy. It is a free strategy as well and she gets a lot of customers from her news stories. She tries to do one per month and with all the different newspapers in her area and this is marketing strategy is powerful enough to bring her enough clients and increase her profits on a month to month basis.

Melanie tells me that one can do the same thing online. Doing news stories like this online is called press releases and one can get over thousand website visitors per day if the press release is done properly and released on the proper place online.

Melanie knows that everyone loves to eat and most people love good food. By offering in home personal cooking lessons, she is attracting plenty of folks who like to spice up their dinner time.

She is not only offering simple cooking lessons, but she specializes in ethnic food recipes and meal plans like Thai food, Oriental food, Mexican food, and European food.

She is emphasizing the uniqueness of her personalized in home cooking classes and she is impressing her clients with her specialized food line cooking courses. Most individuals are going out to dinner for such a unique cuisine.

She has her own website that features articles and recipes about Chinese cuisine, French cuisine, Asian cuisine, Mexican cuisine, etc. to show her clients how to learn how to cook ethnic dishes because Melanie knows that learning to cook ethnic dishes will make any dinner party more impressive and it will turn any dinner time into something unforgettable. Something that everyone is looking forward on a daily basis.

Resources:

http://www.recipesource.com/[1]
http://www.cooksrecipes.com/category/international.html
Fiverr.com[2]
Craigslist.com[3]
Pennysaver.com[4]

---

1. http://www.recipesource.com/
2. http://www.markzuckerbergfortune.info/like/FromPassionToProfit
3. http://pennysaver.com
4. http://pennysaver.com/

Herb Garden Profits

If you love herbs, you must absolutely learn about my friend Michelle who is making lucrative profits from her own herb garden.

Michelle tells me that there is one occupation in the US that is hiring over 1.5 Million people and those

1.5 Million people all need one product.

What is Michelle talking about?

Herb garden profits!

Yes it is true everyone can grow a bushel of money in no time and for pennies.

Let's face it if you go to any decent restaurant and you read the menu, you will notice immediately that nearly every dish is celebrated with fresh herbs. So the question is where do these delicious and aromatic herbs and plants come from?

This is the question that Michelle asked herself when she come up with her own unique food related business idea. The answer is: growing your own beautiful and unique selection of fresh garden herbs!

This is exactly how her idea was born and she has since then been able to grow a very nice herb garden and a nice chunk of change.

Michelle tells me that most herbs are easy to grow and that a luscious herb garden will not only brighten ones yard, but such a garden is very profitable.

Michelle got started her own herb garden by noticing which herbs are the most popular in her area.

Her permanent favorites are mint, parsley, rosemary, basil, cilantro, but there are many more exotic aromatic plants and herbs like lemon grass that is very popular for the Asiatic kitchen.

If you would like to start your own herb garden, you can start exploring sites like

http://www.muextension.missouri.edu/xplor/agguides/hort/g06470.htm

On this site you will learn how to choose your own herbs and how they will grow best. It is a university website that explains what you need to know about herbs.

Next, Michelle recommends to check out the following website:

http://www.w3.aces.uiuc.edu/NRES/extension/factsheets/vc-44/VC-44.html.

It is a great site that gives information on growing herbs in containers. This is the perfect plant garden method if you do not have enough space or if plant eating creatures and bugs are living in your garden.

You need to find the herb seeds or starter plants in order to get started and once you know the best way to raise aromatic herbs and plants.

Mint for example spreads pretty quickly so you do not need to buy lots of seeds. If you are taking good care of your garden and follow the instructions, your garden will very quickly explode on its own and with very little costs.

Once you have your herb garden growing all over the place, what is the next step in order to make a profit from it?

Michelle knows that there are several options that you can choose from.

1. Selling straight to the consumer in a gardener's market stand, or to restaurants.

In this case it is best to take samples of the best herbs and plants to the specific restaurants that you want to sell your herbs to. Make sure to have a pricing sheet prepared. Pricing can be researched well ahead of time.

2. Selling wholesale to grocers.

In this case you can do exactly the same thing as with restaurants, but you will slightly have to lower your pricing.

3. Selling starter plants yourself to other beginning gardeners.

In this case scenario you will require some form of advertising or a simple market stand if your town has a local garden market.

4. Selling out of the back of a pickup truck. In this case make sure that you are allowed to sell like this and that it is legal.

5. Creating the product yourself. Your product line can be anything from oils, herb vinegars to dried plants and herbs.

Use your local library and do your research. Your library will have entire books on this subject.

Michelle is using the internet to find a large number of herb garden growing recipes and it saves her lots of time.

If you have a passion for herbs, you now have all these options that you can work with. It is very enjoyable and easy to see how you can be making lots of profits with your beautiful herb garden.

Michelle is very proud of her own unique herb garden and she is making a very lucrative profit with this green passions. She tells me that as her business is growing, so is her herb garden. It is important to have lots of space for expansions.

Resources:

http://www.muextension.missouri.edu/xplor/agguides/hort/g06470.htm[1]
　http://www.w3.aces.uiuc.edu/NRES/extension/factsheets/vc-44/VC-44.html
　How To Build A Herb Garden[2]
　Building A Herb Garden[3]

---

1. http://www.muextension.missouri.edu/xplor/agguides/hort/g06470.htm
2. 　http://home.howstuffworks.com/how-to-grow-an-herb-garden.htm
3. 　http://www.ehow.com/how_4886121_make-herb-garden.html

Exotic Food Creation Profits

Let's look at another passion to profit story. Genna my foody friend who loves exotic food creations is sharing her own secret ingredients that are key to her unique and successful food creation business.

Genna admits that it is a strange way to make money because it is a way to make money selling something very strange.

Confused?

Genna clarifies and tells me that her business is a business where one needs to think about creating a niche because the business is a niche in itself. There is only one important qualification factor which is the drive to make lots of profit from ones passions.

What is your from passion to profit business model Genna?

It is importing and selling exotic food such as Alligator meat, kangaroo jerky, chocolate covered ants, and many more exotic type of food products.

This will not only satisfy foodies, but dealing with such exotic food products will delight the food aficionados. The food aficionados will love you for serving their platter with something, which is not easily available at their farmer's market on Sundays.

Learning about these exotic food products and their many variations and varieties is the first step.

Make sure to check out the resources below. Genna tells me that she is importing a whole range of exotic foods.

When she got started she started with a narrow range and moved on to find out what is more in demand before adding more varieties to her product line.

When she got started, she utilized the market research already done by current exotic food importing businesses. She started with exploring what types of food products are being offered by local restaurants. She started her own selection process with the biggest restaurants and hotels.

Whenever she is doing her research today, she is using the technology of the internet because most of the big restaurants and hotels have a site online.

She also loves the yellow pages. When doing the initial research, you need to be aware of the 3 basic pieces of information concerning these restaurants and hotels: What exotic food products and what varieties are served, how long has the restaurant/hotel been serving these food products, what are the prices of each food item.

Tip: Always keep all the researched information in well-organized manner i.e. a proper document or a spreadsheet. This will be useful for you in the future

Tip: Once you know which exotic foods would sell best, check the import laws/ restrictions etc. Seek professional advice from someone who is into import-export business.

Procuring the exotic food is the next thing you need to do. The Internet is the best resource to look for various avenues of procurement. There might be a good deal available nearer to you. Check the shipping, packaging, transportation costs, and import duty before arriving at your final cost for procurement. Check the credentials of the company/person you intend to buy from. With all this information in place, you can arrive at the terms that are the best deal for you.

What are the biggest mistakes that one can do with this type of food business?

Never neglect the storage needs for these exotic food products that you are importing and selling the food products is the main challenge of this business.

What is Glenna doing for her marketing?

Glenna has her own website because this gives a more professional look and she can share all her latest information about her food product line on her website.

She also uses local papers for free ads and distributes appealing brochures. The brochures should be distributed at celebration spots and places like food courts, libraries, fairs and other similar places where there is a large influx of people and where a lot of people are hanging out.

She is collaborating with local event organizers for supplying exotic food at parties and local events and occasions. She is keeping them interested by offering a commission.

She is also setting up her stand at local food festivals.

She always hands out her business cards to personal contacts and acquaintances. She uses traditional mouth to mouth marketing, but she also uses social networking hangout places online. She loves business networking places like linkedin.com and she follows one very sneaky online marketing strategy from Dan the Zero Marketing Cost Man that involves a site like meetup.

Trust building and reputation management are very important to her and she uses one of the coolest Zero Cost Marketing reputation strategies online that she learned from Dan's teachings.

The key to success are business contacts and she uses lots of her time to build as many business contacts as she can.

Today Genna is a well known exotic food supplier in her community and she truly lives the from passion into profit lifestyle.

Resources:

Buying alligator meat[1]
> **Buying and learning about exotic meat:**
> http://www.exoticmeats.com
> http://www.foodreference.com/html/artunusualdelicacies.html
> http://www.linkedin.com
> http://www.meetup.com

---

1. http://www.gatorama.com/showpage.asp?page=alligatormeat

Cookbook Profits The Easy Way

Wanna know about my foody friend Sandra who loves to write these unique cookbooks for a huge profit?

If writing is your passion you can easily turn your writing into some cool profits like Sandra is doing it. If you already are a writer, you might consider to research the recipe and cookbook niche because it is truly profitable because women buy lots of cookbooks online. The cookbook niche is more than hot so if you are a writer and your books might not be selling well, you might consider the cookbook niche for your next book project. You will be shocked to see that changing the niche will help you go from zero profits to a very lucrative profit in a very short amount of time.

The cookbook and recipe market is a huge business opportunity, but how do non writers who are passionate about food get started with cookbooks?

The best way to get started is to work from something that already exists and that can be modified in a very creative way to make it stand out and unique.

This type of thinking led Sandra to a very sneaky solution. The solution is to use publications that are in the public domain because early cookbooks do not have any type of copyright and everybody can use them.

When she got started with her business, she did a lot of research and compiling tasks. She says that all of this research work took a lot of time, but she does not regret her work because cookbooks with no copyright are her profit maker number one today.

She is taking the recipes out of these books and creates completely new unique and revised cookbooks. She adds her own creative thinking to the cookbooks like adding some tips, photos, and additional data that is missing and that might turn the recipe into a more valuable and more usable piece of content.

She is letting her publisher know that the recipes were previously published, where they were published, and when they were published.

Sandra loves the saying that the way to a man's heart is through the stomach. She tells me that this is an

age-old saying. Sandra knows that food is something that everyone loves and enjoys; Food is not only enjoyed by men, but it is enjoyed by women and kids as well.

This is the reason why Sandra transformed her passion for food into a profitable business.

Sandra knows that people are always on the lookout for new recipes.

She is always trying out her own recipes on a daily basis. She loves to try out old and new recipes from her huge collection of recipes that she has assembled over the years.

Sandra is mixing her knowledge about the public domain recipe and cookbooks with her own knowledge about food and cooking and comes up with the most creative cookbook concepts and ideas.

She loves to take some time and read these old cookbook recipes and she particularly is interested in the

old fashioned and natural ingredients as well as the different types of preparation methods.

She then matches the knowledge of these public domain type of cookbooks that is beneficial to know about today with her own collection of recipes.

Sandra provides this valuable information on choosing the best ingredients for a dish, which you may not

even have heard or read about anywhere else.

Creating these cookbooks is a very challenging task because some meals are using very interesting ingredients that may sound new and exotic to you. Sandra tells me that these are basically the same basic ingredients that we are using in our kitchen today. They only got a new name to reflect modern times.

Sandra is working on her own research and compiling her research from these old cookbooks and like this she discovers the best old recipes and then brings the content up to date. You do not need to tell your readers about your original public domain source. You only need to inform your publisher about when and where your recipes were originally published.

Sandra tells me that the best places to go and find these types of recipes are all the different libraries that have a big collection of cookbooks. She also asks her grandmother and elderly people if they have kept old cookbooks in their library. Sandra's grandmother loves to cook and she has a huge collection which makes it very easy for Sandra to choose her recipes. She just asks her grandmother about the most interesting recipes and this will help Sandra identify the most delicious tasting recipes that are worth going after.

How does all this publishing stuff work Sandra?

The next big thing is to find an appropriate publisher. She is always approaching very reputable publishers. These publishers might charge a bit more which is worth every penny of it.

She is also using the Kindle publishing platform for self publishing as well as a site called smashwords.

Smashwords is is an e-book self publishing and distribution marketplace.

While Smashwords allows any book author to self publish a book online, like many self publishing providers, Smashwords does not provide some advantages that are typical of traditional and commercial print publishing. Smashword does not provide editing processes, quality control, proof reading, or any book cover design on the site. Smashword authors and publishers provide their manuscripts on an as is basis. Smashwords requires the author to assume responsibilities for the book quality and for their book promotion in the self publishing style.

Smashwords is a self serve publishing service for self publishing authors. Authors are uploading their manuscript as a Microsoft Word files. The Smashwords platform then converts the MS Word files into multiple ebook formats for reading on various e-book reading devices that are available today. Once published by the author, the book is made available for sale online and at a price that has been set by the author. Many traditional book publishers do still publish their ebooks with digital rights management (DRM) copy protection, Smashwords does not use any DRM technology

Futhermore, books published on the Smashwords platform are listed in the Smashwords bookstore. These books are also distributed on the iPhone, the iPod Touch, and the iPad devices via a relationship with a company called Lexcycle. Lexcycle makes the Stanza e-reading app. The content from Smashwords is also being made available through the iBookstore application for the iPad, the iPhone, and the iPod Touch. The complete list of retailers to which Smashwords distributes are the following: Barnes&Noble, Apple iBookstore, Sony, Kobo and the Diesel eBook Store. The Smashwords catalog is also available on Android powered devices for users of the following mobile apps: Kobo, Aldiko, and Word-Player.

Another cool self publishing marketplace for physical cookbooks is a company called Createspace. It is an Amazon company and each book published with Createspace will be available on Amazon as well.

How does the marketing of cookbooks work and what are the secret ingredients to success?

Sandra transforms her cookbooks into ebooks and also sells them on her own site. She also enlists her cookbooks in some of the better directories on the Internet.

She loves to use Dan the Zero Cost Marketing guy's Pinterest marketing strategy and she submits photos of delicious food dishes to Pinterest and leads her visitors back to her own website from where she sells her unique cookbooks.

She also places ads on websites related to cooking and food. Like this people who visit these sites may get interested in buying her beautifully and unique designed, and written cookbooks.

This story brings me to yet another similar best selling cookbook author story that I will be covering in the next chapter of this book.

Resources:

Foodhistory.com[1]

---

[1] http://www.foodhistory.com

Become A Foody Authority & Best Selling Author With Food Deliciousness

My good friend Lillie is sharing another from passion into profit foody story with me. She is passionately telling me her story of how she became a foody authority and best selling author with food deliciousness.

Let's hear her story.

You may be thinking cookbooks have been done, but after having listened to Lillie's story I know for a fact that people are always looking for new cookbook concepts and with different themed recipes that provide a valuable solution for them.

Did you know that many health minded people or those who are on specific diets, whether for health reasons or just to lose weight, are also looking for a solution that is going to provide them with delicious recipes while helping them with their weight loss problems.

And no you do not have to be a master chef to become a best selling author with food neither.

She tells me that it is very important to create a truly attractive and useful cookbook with lots of appeal for the right type of target customers. Once her creation process has been done, she starts thinking about the right marketing strategy for her book.

She is always designing her cookbook in a way so that it stands out among her competitors. This is extremely important she says. There are many cookbooks available to consumers and this is why you have to make them want to pick yours up first.

The most important thing is the title. She spends most of the time coming up with a catchy cookbook title and a unique hook that is going to do the selling of the cookbook for you and upon first glance.

The content of the cookbook is the true challenge because the content within it will be the next thing they look at.

She likes to come up with theme based cookbook concepts like providing a host of meal ideas based upon healthier ideas of eating, and recipes to help lose weight, and quick & easy to make meals, microwave meals, slowcooker meals, dinner meal plans for each week night, recipes for busy moms, caveman type recipe books, recipes for under $10, non bake cake recipes, 5 minute type recipes,

recipes that are based on specific ingredients, and photo cook books that are based on only one delicious recipe that is documented via a load of photos to show the whole cooking process.

Lillie also likes to make cookbooks that include all the meals within the cookbook and the extras as well. These things should include breakfast recipes that are exciting, inventive, nutritious, and appealing type of breakfast recipes and that will make any breakfast-time a healthy one. This will help anyone seeking healthier life styles know which things they should include within their diet.

She makes other cookbooks that include lunch and dinner recipes. Lunches can be anywhere from light to heavy and geared towards the family or just one person.

Another great idea for cookbooks are specific cookbooks on the topic of snacks, deserts, and beverages.

When it comes to healthy type recipe cookbooks one common myth for those that are trying to lose weight is that the food must be bland and tasteless, in order to be successful. This could not be further from the truth and by creating her own cookbooks, Lillie can help put this myth aside.

Lastly, Lillie creates another type of cookbook that bases the recipes around meal plans that will help people develop their diet plans easier and perhaps with better nutrition. Meal plans are meals that she is outlining in her cookbook and it goes from breakfast to dinner and anywhere in between.

Lillie is a very creative cookbook writer and she keeps telling me that there is a huge variety of ideas that one could incorporate into cookbook art, design, and content.

Can you give an example for such a cookbook?

She tells me that she loves to do these cookbooks that include measurement chart for measuring ingredients. She also includes the calories with each serving of the meals that she is providing. The whole

concept is to make the cookbook appealing and useful to the targeted audience. This in itself coupled with advertising of the cookbook is helping her create very satisfying and lucrative cookbooks.

Below Lillie is sharing some useful and valuable resources to help you get started as a best selling cookbook author.

Resources

http://www.free-gourmet-recipes.com [1]
  http://www.recipetrove.com

---

[1] http://www.free-gourmet-recipes.com

About the Publisher

InfinitYou is a hybrid general interest trade publisher. One of the first of its kind InfinitYou publishes physical books, electronic books, and audiobooks in various genres. Our publications are meant to educate, edify and entertain readers of all walks of life from babies to the elderly. Home to more than twenty imprints such as Infinit Baby, Infinit Kids, Infinit Girl, Infinit Boy, Infinit Coloring, Infinit Swear Words, Infinit Activities, Infinit Productivity, Infinit Cat, Infinit Dog, Infinit Love, Infinit Family, Infinit Survival, Infinit Health, Infinit Beauty, Infinit Spirituality, Infinit Lifestyle, Infinit Wealth, Infinit Romance, and lots more.

www.ingramcontent.com/pod-product-compliance
Lightning Source LLC
LaVergne TN
LVHW020455080526
838202LV00057B/5974